PRAYERS
FOR DEPRESSION

Also by Fay Sampson:

Prayers for Dementia: And how to live well with it

PRAYERS
FOR DEPRESSION
And how to best live with it

FAY SAMPSON

DARTON · LONGMAN + TODD

First published in Great Britain in 2017 by
Darton, Longman and Todd Ltd
1 Spencer Court
140–142 Wandsworth High Street
London SW18 4JJ

ISBN 978-0-232-53295-1

A catalogue record for this book is available from the British
Library.

Designed and produced by Judy Linard
Printed and bound in Great Britain by Bell and Bain, Glasgow

ABOUT THIS BOOK

Depression is an illness which can creep up on us before we realize it. It is not uncommon to feel low at times. It's when days stretch out into weeks, and it is having a negative effect on your life, that you need to take it seriously.

It can take many forms. This book offers information and advice about different aspects of the condition, and what can be done to help. Each page of advice is accompanied by a relevant prayer.

The prayers are divided into two groups. The first is for the use of those with depression, or on their behalf. The second is for family, friends and the wider community.

When praying for someone, you may wish to insert *him, her* or a personal name, in place of the more general pronoun *they*.

My warm thanks are due to Mind.UK, Depression. UK and the many people whose personal testimonies of depression have helped to shape this book.

At the end there is a list of helpful resources. You can find many more on the Mind.UK website. There is also space to add your own.

Half the royalties from this book will go to Mind UK.

Though I walk through the valley
of the shadow of death,
thou art with me;
Thy rod and thy staff,
they comfort me.

Psalm 23

PART A

For the use of, or on behalf of, those with depression

THE DARK CLOUD

People with depression often speak of feeling they are surrounded by a dark cloud. It cuts them off from everything which used to make life enjoyable and meaningful. Because nothing gives them satisfaction or pleasure, there seems no point in doing anything. It's not even worth getting out of bed.

Try to concentrate on the little things. Hard though it is, it is important that you go through the motions. It matters that you get up in the morning. You need to make yourself a simple breakfast, even though you don't have an appetite. The way you are feeling, each of these small successes becomes a great achievement. You can pat yourself on the back.

Prayer, too, may seem like going through the motions. But it's not wasted time. Its usefulness doesn't depend on the feel-good factor.

In the Gospels we read of the man at the Pool of Bethesda. Every day he dragged himself there, hoping to be cured of his disability. But he had no one to help him. When the healing spring bubbled up, he couldn't get into the water in time. Yet, day after day, he kept going, even though it seemed hopeless. Because he was there, Jesus saw his need and offered him his own healing.

Keeping going, even in small steps, is part of getting well.

Lord, I know I ought to pray.

I *need* to pray. . .

I can't pray.

I sit in the usual place. I open my Bible. I try to focus my mind on you. . .

Nothing happens.

I feel as though nobody is there.

I am surrounded by a grey cloud. I can see nothing beyond it. I feel nothing. I hope for nothing.

There seems no point.

Nothing that used to delight me gives me pleasure. I don't want to see my friends. I have no appetite for my favourite food. Trying to pray to you seems meaningless. No one will hear me.

I'm just going through the motions.

If you are really there, somewhere beyond this greyness, have pity on me.

I used to think that the Holy Spirit blew through the world like the wind of God. I beg you to tear this cloud apart and let in your heavenly Light.

Lord, help me. Help my unbelief.

FEELING WORTHLESS

It is common for people suffering depression to lose their sense of self-worth.

The condition may be triggered by some form of rejection: losing your job, failing an exam, the break-up of a relationship with someone you loved. You are made to feel that there is something wrong with you. You are not good enough.

It's natural to feel low afterwards. Anyone would.

But you need to be concerned if the pain has gone so deep that you feel you haven't just failed in this one thing, but that your whole life is a failure.

When you have been knocked so low, it's hard to start to pick yourself up and look at the positives. If depression has got hold of you, it can make things worse in other areas. If you still have a job, or a study course, or a relationship, then your depression about one thing may make you want to withdraw from others. You give up trying, you retreat within yourself. More things begin to go wrong. Your sense of failure can become a self-fulfilling prophecy.

The one thing which is most difficult to do if you are depressed is to 'snap out of it'. If only you could.

As so often when things are hard, start with small things. Look back over your life. There have been high points, haven't there? See if you can find a photograph or some other memento which reminds you of that. When were you happy? When did you do something you felt good about? That time was real, even if you don't feel like that now. If it was true once, it can be true again in the future.

Make a box of your 'positives'. Open it when you feel down. Relive your times of joy. One day, you can be again the 'you' you were then.

Christ, Saviour of Sinners,

I know I need to ask your help, but I don't feel I'm worthy to come before you.

I know I'm a failure. I can see it in the faces all around me. I can't do my job properly. I'm rude or surly to my friends. I can't sort myself out, let alone help anyone else. Why should you bother with me? Why should anyone?

Sometimes I think I should just let go and die. Who would miss me? The way I am, I'm just a waste of space.

But then I remember Calvary. I see you hanging there. I see the blood running down your side. I see your head bowed in agony. I hear your words of desolation: 'My God, why have you forsaken me?'

And I know you have been through a darker vale than mine. You let yourself be mocked and spat upon and crucified.

The amazing thing is that you did it for people like me. Not just for the good people. Not just for the heroes. Not just for the ones who are giving their lives to serve your kingdom. You died for the worthless, for the failures, for the guilty. You died for me.

In the blackness of the way I feel about myself, this is the one thing I can hang on to. You value me. You love me. You thought I was worth dying for.

WORK

Most of us find work stressful to some degree. Usually we can cope with it. We even grow stronger from meeting challenges and overcoming them.

It can be devastating to suddenly find yourself unable to cope. You've lost the ability to make decisions. You feel paralysed. You think your colleagues are talking behind your back about your inadequacy to do the job. You just want to hide away.

It may have been triggered by some setback or small failure. Everyone has these. It's not the end of the world. But it's made you lose confidence in yourself.

There may have been a change in staffing. The good relationships you relied on are no longer there. There may now be someone you find it hard to get along with. You feel adrift and alone.

You feel that home should be your refuge. This should be the place where you are valued and comforted. You don't want to leave it in the morning.

Then you get home and find a host of demands you are not ready to meet. Your partner has problems and wants to talk about them. Something needs doing to the house. You are asked to make decisions. You just can't cope with any more. You hit back at the very person you hoped would help you.

If you have children, they won't understand the way you are feeling. They are insistent in their demands. You snap at them, and make it worse.

Home is no longer the refuge you need it to be. Despair threatens to take over.

The best thing you can do is talk about it. Don't try to keep up the façade of being the strong one. Admit your weakness, and the way you feel. The very act of talking about your feelings is a way of bringing them under control.

Christ, my Master,

I used to be good at my job. I was the one who made plans. I took decisions.

Now I want to hide behind the office door, or in the toilets. I can't face the demands of the job. I can't make decisions any more.

When I think of going to work in the morning, I fear I am going to be sick.

I used to be strong. My partner leaned on me. The children looked up to me.

Now I can't cope with the demands they make on me. I don't want to listen to my partner. I snap at the children.

I don't understand what is happening to me. I don't recognise the person I have become.

I don't even feel there is much point praying to you. I hear a voice saying: 'What good will it do?' You're not going to wave a magic wand and make me better.

But where else can I turn? I'm desperate for someone to help me get through the day.

Desperate people came to you. You touched them and healed them.

Reach out to me in my feeling of failure and hopelessness. Allow me to confess my weakness. Comfort me.

THE BURIED PAST

Depression can hit you out of the blue. There is no obvious cause. The roots may lie buried so far back in your past that you haven't recognised them.

It could be childhood abuse, a bereavement that hit you harder than you realised, a broken relationship, a failure you thought you had got over. Something may have happened recently to trigger that buried memory. There are issues that have never been properly dealt with. You take refuge from them under the blanket of depression.

It's hard to deal with something which has never been brought out into the open. Even now, your depression may be shutting out the acknowledgement of what this is.

This is where talking to someone can be invaluable. As you respond to sympathetic prompts you may find yourself talking through that forgotten episode. It's easier to come to terms with something you can see face to face.

With some aspects of depression, talking to a friend can be a great help. This sort of thing, however, is best done with a skilled professional. Go to your doctor. Tell them how you are feeling and that there seems no obvious cause. You may have to go on a waiting list for talking therapy, but it's worth persevering. You want your old life back, don't you?

God, who knows my secrets better than I do myself,

I put myself into your hands.

I cannot find the reason for my depression. All I know is that my life has become unbearable.

I give you thanks that there are those who care about my condition. People who are willing to listen to me. Those who want to take my hand and lead me to the discovery of what is wrong with me.

Save me from the despair which says that no one can help me. Counter the cynicism which says it's not worth waiting months. As the weeks stretch out, sometimes I can't find the will to want to get better.

I know that finding out what has caused my depression may be painful. Give me the courage to have old wounds re-opened. Let me know myself honestly, so that I can co-operate with my healing.

I need your strength and your comfort. Give me courage.

MEDICATION AND DRUGS

If you are experiencing depression there are a variety of possible causes. Some of these are chemical. Your depression may be related to medication you are taking. It could be the result of alcohol or street drugs.

If you regularly take medication of any sort, check the leaflet. Does it list depression as a possible side effect? If so, it's an easy matter to go to your doctor and explain how you are feeling. They can probably change your prescription without causing you such distress. They may be able to offer other help as well.

Depression can also be brought about by alcohol or street drugs. You may be tempted to drink more if you are feeling low. Mind UK has a detailed list of different recreational drugs and their possible effects on you. Check out any drugs you use and see if this relates to you.

Not everyone reacts in the same way to drugs. You may have friends who enjoy their use with no apparent ill effects. You are a unique individual. There may be factors in your make-up, or in your experience, which make you particularly vulnerable.

Seek help. You may be messing up your life, or doing long-term damage, if you let it go on. Discuss it with your doctor. You may be given a support worker who can help you make changes in your lifestyle. There are self-help groups, where people sharing your experience can help each other get through it.

Don't hold back because you may have been using an illegal substance. This is not about being judgemental; it's about healing you.

Creator God,

you made my body and now it's in a mess. I feel terrible.

Give me the courage to lay my problems before someone who can help me. Take away the fear that they will judge me.

Grant me the courage to make the changes I need to be whole again. Let me trust in the support of those who want to heal me. Walk beside me through the difficult path of change.

I look around the world. I am overwhelmed by gratitude that so much help is available to me here. Even in the depths of my depression, help me to reach out and take it.

Let me not be selfish in my suffering. I pray for all the thousands who are going through the same depression. Grant me the grace to share my experience with them, so that together we may find the way to wholeness. May I support them when they falter, and gratefully accept the strength they offer me in return.

I pray for my family and my friends. I know my condition has not been easy for them. Let me not be selfish in clinging on to the way I have abused my body. In your loving pity, reach out and help me to be the person they want me to be.

Walk beside me. I cannot do it alone.

GETTING HELP

It's difficult for other people to understand how paralyzing depression is. They can see that you are ill. They know that you need help. To them, it seems a simple matter to phone the surgery and make an appointment and then to go along and see your doctor.

But you shrink from making contact with the outside world. You expect to be laughed at, rejected. Telling your troubles to someone you hardly know feels impossible. You don't believe it will work.

Take hold of the fact that depression is a real illness. Your doctor knows that. They will have seen many more cases like you. They *will* take you seriously.

You don't really want your whole life to drag on like this, do you? It needn't. People who have suffered depression for years come out on the other side of it. They pick up normal lives again. They hold down a job. They have friends, a social life. You'd like that, wouldn't you?

Depression isn't a life sentence. There are things that can really help. A good one is talking therapy, which can come in a variety of forms. You may have to wait for a place, but it's worth persevering.

There is medication. You and your doctor may need to experiment a bit to find which one works best for you.

You may be experiencing more severe symptoms, such as delusions or bipolar disorder. Your doctor can discuss the treatments available.

You may find that your mood varies. Sometimes you are stuck under this great grey cloud that you can't escape. At other times you feel nearer to your normal self. Take advantage of these lighter times to pick up the phone and make that appointment.

It may help to tell a friend or a family member that

you have done so. They can help you get up your nerve to keep that appointment.

Help is out there. You are not alone.

Lord, Helper of the lost,

in my clearer moments I know I should ask for help. That's what everyone tells me. 'Go and see your doctor.'

Then the gloom closes in again. How can anyone else understand the way I am feeling? They'll tell me 'Take more exercise. Eat healthy food. Get out more.'

How can I explain the crushing weight I feel? You'd think those simple things would be easy to do, but every little move takes such an enormous effort. I imagine sitting in a doctor's waiting room, trying to think how to explain what's wrong with me. It seems impossible and futile.

But I'm not getting any better. I'm beginning to fear that the rest of my life will be like this. I need help.

Take me by the hand. Let me feel the strength of your grip close around mine. Nerve me to make an appointment and then to keep it. Sit beside me as I wait for my name to be called. Give me honesty to say exactly how I feel.

In my worst moments, I can't even imagine how it would feel to be well.

Guide me to where healing can begin.

KNOWLEDGE

There is a saying: 'Know your enemy'.

Depression can feel like a life sentence. The more you understand about your condition, the more likely you are to get back to your normal self.

Even if you are in that state where you don't want to venture outdoors, you can still use a computer. There are stacks of information available. You can share other people's experience of depression. Go to www.mind.org.uk and click on 'Depression'.

If you are not into online searches yourself, then ask a friend to print out those information pages or order booklets for you.

Depression may inhibit you from picking up the phone, but if you feel up to it, their infoline is 0300 123 3393. You will find someone sympathetic and knowledgeable on the other end of the line.

Check which symptoms of depression apply to you. Read the many possible causes. Does anything ring a bell? If so, it would help to share this with your doctor.

There is lots of advice about things that can help you feel better. Depression can make you lethargic about taking positive steps. Start with one small thing.

You will read about the range of treatments available. Each of us is a unique individual. It will take some experimentation to find what works best for you. Allow your doctor to take part in your healing. You are not likely to get better if you just sit at home and do nothing. You don't really want to stay as you are, do you?

The Mind website has a long list of other sources where you can get help. These may deal specifically with one aspect of depression which applies to you.

Depression UK brings together local groups for self

help. Depression can make you feel alone and hopeless. It can be both a relief and an inspiration to get together with others who are sharing the same experience and find what works for them. See: www.depressionuk.org.

Crucified Christ,

you underwent this painful and shameful death so that there would be no depth of our suffering you could not share.

Open my eyes to all the others who suffer from depression as I do.

Though I am tempted to despair, I give thanks that so much help and information is available for me. I am full of gratitude that so many people devote their lives to those of us who suffer in this way.

Save me from being so overwhelmed with self pity that I won't even look at what is available. Let me at least find out more about what is wrong with me, what may have caused it. You know how hard it is for me to turn outward, feeling the way I do. Yet inspire me with a little of your compassion for my fellow-sufferers. Show me what I can do to share my experiences and learn from them.

We are all part of the one Body which is you. When one of us hurts, all of us do. Give me the grace to help others towards healing too.

CREATIVITY

Creative artists are more prone to depression or bipolar disorder than the population as a whole. Think of Beethoven, Virginia Woolf, Isaac Newton. This may be because their chosen discipline turns their thoughts inwards more than most.

Yet creativity can also be a help for those suffering from depression. Many of those who experience it say that there is a feeling of relief, even that rare thing: happiness, when they pick up a paint brush, finger their guitar, write a poem.

Contemplating beauty causes chemical changes in the brain. Use that uplift to enhance your own pleasure. Time spent on the creative arts can be part of your healing.

Depression makes it hard for you to communicate with other people. There is no such barrier with music, drama, dance, painting, sculpture, or writing. The materials you use to express yourself won't judge you. With or without words, they let you say what you feel.

The art form doesn't have to be about your depression, although it can be. Just enjoy the beauty in whatever way you like. Let yourself go. For a little while, be happier.

If you want to take it deeper, there are art therapy courses. A trained professional, with a love and understanding of that particular art, can help you come to terms with your disorder through this self-expression. Your hands, your eyes, your body, may say more surely what your tongue cannot.

Creating God,

when my world is so often dull and colourless, I give you thanks that I can find release and joy in creativity. Weighed down though I am with depression, I can still create something of beauty.

So often, the dark feelings I have are trapped inside me. I know I should talk to someone about this, but I can't find the right person, the right time, the right words. Yet the gifts you have given me speak for me. As I engage in my chosen art, I feel some of the weight lift from me.

You threw the stars into space. You fling the waves in spray against the rocks. You sing to me in the skylark's music. You must know how I feel, generous Creator.

When the night is darkest, when I can see no end to this tunnel, lift my soul with the remembrance of things beautiful. May my small act of creation find a joyful echo in your heart.

PANIC ATTACKS

People experiencing depression may be subject to panic attacks. Your heart is racing. You think you are going to faint. You may feel sweaty, with shaking limbs, or seized with sickness. You have difficulty breathing, or you hyperventilate. You may even fear you are going to die.

You need help.

One of the things that works best is to talk it over with someone you trust. This could be a friend, or you might contact a group such as Anxiety UK. Your doctor will recognize this as one symptom of your illness and can suggest help.

Understanding what is happening can be key to overcoming it. Try to remember if there is any common factor that seems to trigger these attacks. This is where talking it through can help.

Getting to the root of these attacks is the surest step to getting well. You may think your fears are irrational, but there is probably a good reason for them.

There are simple things you can do to help. Breathing exercises help you to control one of the common features of a panic attack: difficulty in breathing normally. Physical exercise will help, as will eating a healthy diet. You may find both of these particularly difficult if you are suffering from depression. Everything seems such an effort. Set yourself small, achievable goals, and pat yourself on your back when you reach them. Go easy on caffeine and sugar. Listening to music you enjoy can be a helpful therapy.

The arms of God are waiting to give you reassurance. Lean on Him.

Heavenly Father, I'm scared.

I wake up at night with a panic attack. It's not a nightmare. It doesn't disappear as soon as I'm awake. The thing I am afraid of is there with me in the room. I can't get away from it. I can't run. I'm drenched with sweat and shaking. My heart is pounding.

I can't leave it behind me even in the daytime. I am terrified of being terrified. What if it strikes me when I'm out on the street, in a shop, at work?

It's one more reason to stay indoors. I can't get away from the feeling I am so afraid of, but at least no one else will see my shame.

I know you were afraid. In the Garden of Gethsemane you sweated your fear like drops of blood. Help me.

FOOD

Food can be a problem when you are depressed.

The colour and joy have gone out of life. You have lost interest in things that used to give you pleasure. It doesn't seem worth getting yourself a proper meal. Sometimes you may not be bothered to eat at all.

Or else you are tense and anxious. It feels as though a hand is tightening round your throat. You're sure that, if you try to eat anything, you will be sick.

Or you might go to the other extreme. You feel so rotten that you take refuge in bingeing on comfort food. Putting on weight will just make you feel worse.

The right food is important, not just for physical health, for mental wellbeing. The trouble is that you feel so lethargic or despairing that you have stopped looking after yourself. And that is making you worse.

How can you break out of this vicious circle?

The fundamental thing you need to convince yourself of is that you matter. However hopeless you feel about yourself, you are really precious. There are other people out there who care about you. They have a vision of the person you were and can be. They see you healthy, lively, enjoying life. They believe in you.

Give yourself permission to love yourself.

Take a good look at yourself in a full-length mirror. Is this the person you want to be for the rest of your life?

As with so many things in handling depression, set yourself small goals at first. Write down a list of your favourite foods. Now, rearrange that list with the healthier foods at the top.

Make up your mind to eat at least one of those every day. It need only be a small portion.

Eat slowly. Take time to savour the food and enjoy

it. Picture the good it is doing you. When you have finished, congratulate yourself.

You matter.

Lord of enjoyment,

how often we see you at the table of your friends and followers. You were a man people wanted to invite to a meal.

I invite you now to my table. I see your concern at the way I have been feeding myself – or not feeding. This isn't the food I would put before you as my guest.

Give me the grace to value myself as much as you value me. I don't think I'm worth bothering about, so it doesn't seem to matter what, or if, I eat. Astonish me with the love in your eyes which tells me I am uniquely precious.

Let me see my body with new eyes. This is the temple of my spirit. May I see it as you do, as I could be, renewed and healthy. Grant me the conviction that I can be well, and that good food is part of that healing.

Sit by my side as I take small advances towards changing my way of life. Don't let me give up. Be patient with me when I fail, and fall back into bad habits. Renew my determination to be what you want me to be, what I can be.

Bring the enjoyment of life-giving food back into my colourless life. And share that enjoyment with me.

EXERCISE

You know that you need fresh air and exercise. It's not doing you any good, cowering away from the world indoors. Exercise changes the body's chemistry. You will come back feeling happier and more positive.

Yet knowing is not the same as bridging the gap between this room, where you feel gloomy but safe, and the outside world which seems to have turned against you. It takes courage to step over the threshold.

You really don't want to make the effort.

It can feel as though depression is a life sentence. You can't see past the gloom to a time when you will feel normal again. Yet the world abounds with people who have been through depression and are now leading happy and successful lives.

Healing is there. But it needs you to co-operate.

That's easy to say. It can feel enormously difficult to do.

Set yourself small, achievable goals. You don't have to embark on a punishing regime. You might begin with a few exercises, right here in your room. Concentrate on your breathing; that can help too. If you are into yoga, that can be beneficial to both your spirit and your body.

If you go to work, to college, to the shops, walk briskly.

If things have got so bad that you are no longer doing these things, then persuade yourself to make one foray out of doors each day. It could be walking, cycling, swimming — whatever you enjoy. It may be just a walk around the block, or a mile's cycle ride. So long as it gets the heartbeat up and the breathing deeper. Savour the experience. Make enjoyment a reality. Feel your muscles work and the wind on your face. It's a gift, not a penance.

And it really will help your healing.

Journeying Christ, who walked the stony roads of Palestine in search of those who needed you,

forgive me those days when I can't even get out of bed.

I know that I ought to exchange the fug of this room for your wind, your sunshine, your fresh air outdoors. I know that I will feel better for the exercise, that I will come back refreshed.

And yet, it is though there is a barrier at the door. I can't even persuade myself to get properly dressed. My head tells me exercise will be good for me. My instincts rebel against it.

Be patient with me. Don't give up on me. Take me by the hand. Fill me with the courage to get through that door.

Give me a vision of what it will be like: the pavement under my feet, the pedals turning, the flow of water past my body as I swim. Let me hold on to the joy of movement. Make that vision come true.

You rose before dawn and walked out into the hills to be with your Father. It can't be so difficult for me to get out for half an hour, can it?

I find myself shrinking from even this small effort.

Help me, travelling God.

PERSEVERANCE

Sadly, there is no quick and easy cure for depression. There are a large number of possible causes and a variety of treatments. Finding which of these fits your own case may take time.

It can be hard to motivate yourself to seek help, and harder still to keep going when there are no obvious results.

If you really want to get better, you will need to work through some of these possibilities with your doctor.

You may be prescribed an antidepressant. These are not a magic cure for depression, but they can lift your mood so that you are able to make better use of other forms of treatment and changes in lifestyle.

There are nearly thirty different kinds. They can have varying side effects. You may have a different experience with one than someone else does. Be patient. Tell your doctor about any unpleasant reaction. Switching to another type may work better for you. You may have to try several before you find the one which is right for you. This doesn't mean they are a waste of time. It's a matter of trial and error.

Talking therapies can be very useful. A professional can help you talk through the possible causes of your depression. In the process, you may find you are discovering your own path to healing.

But waiting lists can be long. Tell yourself that, without help, depression can go on for years. Don't let it steal too much of your life. Waiting a few months can save you years of misery.

And when the therapy begins, it's not a quick fix. Don't give up because you don't get instant results. Your life is precious. It's worth taking time to get it right.

And while you wait to sort out your treatment, there is lots you can do. Exercise, diet, talking to family or friends. It's a long road, but you don't have to walk it alone.

Patient God,
you have put up with us for millennia. Forgive me if I fret over a few weeks delay.

You know how hard it was for me to take the first step. Protect me from frustration when I can't see immediate results.

Let me trust the doctors and support workers who are trying their best to bring me healing. When I want to give up, remind me how much of their time I would be throwing away.

I find the misery of depression unbearable, and yet sometimes I despair of ever being better.

Help me. May your inspiring Spirit fill me with hope. May the Christ who trod the hard road to Calvary give me strength. May your loving arms reassure me that one day I will be whole.

ALTERNATIVE THERAPIES

There are a number of conventional treatments available for depression. There is a wide range of medication. There are talking therapies of various kinds.

There are also alternative treatments. These are not clinically proven, but some people find they help. You may want to try one while you wait to find the right medication or for talking therapy to begin.

For mild depression, some find relief in mindfulness. You become more aware of your thoughts and feelings. You give your full attention to the present moment: mind, body, surroundings. It can help you feel calmer, and replace unhelpful thoughts with more positive ones. You will need to commit to regular practice to get real benefit.

There are a number of other choices: yoga, acupuncture, aromatherapy, herbal remedies, and so on. Mind UK has a comprehensive list. The aim of these is to help you feel relaxed and relieve your stress.

Exercise programmes can give you a feeling of wellbeing and make you feel more in control of things. A course in an expressive art may provide an outlet for your feelings.

In extreme cases, you may be offered ECT (electroconvulsive therapy). This is only appropriate when you have had severe depression for a long time and it's not responding to other treatments, or if your condition has become life-threatening. You will need to have an informed discussion with your doctor.

There are so many possibilities. Depression will tempt you not to make the effort. But you don't want to waste years of your life for lack of trying. You may even find you enjoy one of these.

God of the open hands and boundless love,

even in the darkness of depression, I give you thanks that there are so many ways of healing available.

Yet you know how hard it is for me to make even a small effort. The weight I feel tempts me to feel it is all hopeless. I can't imagine a time when I will feel normal again.

Touch me with the inspiration of your Spirit and give me hope. Enable me to reach out towards life. Grant me the grace to enjoy the pleasure of activities which will help me feel better.

I feel the life I have now is worthless. But you love me. You believe in me. You laid down your life for me. I *do* have worth.

Help me to take up that offer of life.

PRE- AND POST-NATAL DEPRESSION

It's normal to feel overjoyed when your baby is born. It's also common to experience a sag in your emotions a few days later. If it's your first baby, you are having to cope with a radical change in your lifestyle. If there are other children, you have to juggle your responsibilities both to the new baby and to them. The flood of congratulations has petered out. You are not getting a good night's sleep. You're on your own.

The majority of new parents recover from this naturally. They learn how to cope.

But a significant minority find these symptoms don't go away. They feel weighed down by the baby's demands. They feel inadequate to deal with them. They may find themselves indifferent to the baby, or even hostile to it. They feel tired all the time. They look at other mothers and feel a failure.

If this is happening to you, you are suffering from post-natal depression. As with any other illness, you need help. Initially, this may be medication to lift your mood. Further down the line, there may be talking therapy. Comparing notes with other depressed mothers can help. You really aren't alone. You're a minority, but you are not abnormal.

You can feel these symptoms even before the baby is born. You feel overwhelmed by the prospect in front of you. This is pre-natal depression. Untreated, it can spoil what should be a wonderful experience.

It happens most frequently with mothers, but it can affect fathers too. They also feel the weight of sleepless nights, the extra financial responsibility, the realisation of how much a baby will change their lifestyle.

You may be particularly at risk if you have previously

suffered a mental illness, if there is some trauma in your childhood background, if you have recently suffered bereavement, loss of job, or some other major setback.

Your baby needs you, but you too need help.

Mothering God,

I don't understand what is happening to me. I so much wanted this baby. This should have been one of the greatest joys of my life.

Instead, I feel defeated and afraid.

I can't cope with the responsibility of a living child. What will I do if something goes wrong? I'm afraid to touch my baby, in case I hurt it.

I don't feel any of the love I expected to. I'd rather not be in the same room as this child. I want someone to take it away and leave me alone.

Why am I such a colossal failure? Other mothers seem to take to it naturally. I see their pride and their happiness, and I can't feel any of that.

Dear God, I'm the one who needs parenting. I want your caring arms around me. I want you to assure me that I'm not unnatural. That you won't turn your love away from me because I can't find love in my own heart for this child.

Accept my tears and my feelings of worthlessness.

Give me back the joy of this precious gift.

SELF-HARM AND SUICIDE

Feelings of depression can be so severe that you want to hurt yourself. You may cut your body, take poison, neglect your well-being, resort to physically punishing exercise. In extreme cases, you may even want to kill yourself.

It may help to keep a log of these events. Does a pattern emerge of things that seem to trigger such feelings? Have there been painful reminders of things in your past? Is there a person who provokes this reaction? Does it happen in certain situations, or at a particular time of day? Understanding this urge is a step towards relieving it.

Give yourself alternative ways to express your violent feelings. Thump a cushion. Yell. Tear up a newspaper. Find an outlet in creative art or dance, where you can pour out how you feel.

If self-harm feels like a way of regaining control over the mess of depression, think of another method. Tidy a cupboard. Wash some clothes. Make a list of things you need to do.

If it's not anger you are feeling, but sadness and fear of a hostile world, be good to yourself. Wrap up warmly and curl up on a sofa with a cup of something hot. Play comforting music. Go for a leisurely walk in beautiful surroundings.

Talk to someone. There are helplines. The Samaritans, Mind UK, and many more. Add their numbers to your contacts. You may feel it's just you against the world, but there are thousands who feel as you do.

Find someone you can talk to: a friend, a family member, a counsellor. You don't have to walk this dark way alone.

Pray.

Wounded Christ,

I look at the marks on my body with shame. These are not the scars of love like yours, but the wounds of hate. I feel worthless, in need of punishment.

This is not the person you want me to be.

I confess that when I did this to myself I felt a bit better. It released some of the anger, the frustration. I turn to you in desperation. Show me another way. Give me the strength to follow that different path.

I know what others will think about me if they see these scars. They will say I am seeking attention.

You alone understand that sometimes I can't help myself. I have this overwhelming desire to hurt myself. Catch my hands and hold me back.

Breath of God, grant me that breathing space, the moment when I could make a different choice.

You're the only one who doesn't think I'm worthless. You died for me, and I am precious in your sight.

That's too wonderful for me to take in, the way I'm feeling about myself right now. Just help me to begin.

In your love, may I love myself.

LAUGHTER

Laughter is not something we readily associate with depression. Yet it can be surprisingly therapeutic. Even the act of smiling can make us feel happier. Try it.

Be nice to yourself. Think of films or programmes that make you laugh or give you pleasure. Put your feet up and enjoy one.

Sometimes it can help you to release your feelings of anger or misery in creative work. But try another approach as well. Think of things you have found pleasurable or beautiful in the past. You may find it difficult to summon up those same feelings just now, but let your memory go to work. Express those good feelings in art, poetry, dance, whatever suits you. It doesn't have to be brilliant. It's just you being you. And enjoying life was once an important part of who you are.

At times, you feel you are under a dark cloud, and you can't get out from beneath it. But there are sometimes better days, when the gloom lightens a little. Make the most of them. Step back and look at yourself. Sloppily dressed, picking at your food, not bothering enough about personal hygiene, surly with your friends. *Is that really me?* All right, you're allowed a measure of self-pity. Depression is no joke. But couldn't you, just sometimes, smile at the caricature of yourself you have become?

Allow yourself the luxury of pleasure, beauty, comedy, fun. You may feel worse again tomorrow, but let the light in while you can.

Lord of Laughter,

who told so many jokes in your parables, help me not always to take myself too seriously, even though laughing is the last thing I feel like doing.

Help me to seize on those lighter moments and give myself the refreshment of comedy and enjoyment.

I know I am a miserable companion to my friends and family most of the time. I'm a miserable companion to myself. Give me the grace to accept the invitation they offer me to go out and enjoy myself once in a while.

Comfort me with films and TV, with art and music. Allow me to be kind to myself.

I know you will walk this long, dark road with me. Lighten the gloom for me sometimes with the magic of your smile.

PART B

For the use of family, friends
and the wider community

THE WARNING SIGNS

Someone suffering from depression is unlikely to take themselves to their doctor and report it. It may take some time to recognize that the dispiriting change in their feelings is an illness. It may fall to caring family members or friends to realize that all is not well.

Has the person you care about changed their behaviour? Have they stopped socializing in ways they used to enjoy? Do they seem withdrawn, tired, dejected? Is their appetite poor? Do they seem more reliant on alcohol or other drugs than they used to be?

They may have stopped coming out any more. They don't respond to your messages. By now you should be seriously concerned.

You may be the person they need to help them take decisive action, when they no longer feel able to do that for themselves.

Find out about depression and its symptoms. Visit the Mind website. Talk this through with them. If this seems to match the way they are feeling, then advise them to see their doctor. If this seems too much of an effort for them, or they feel hopeless about its usefulness, help them to make an appointment. Arrange to pick them up and accompany them to the surgery.

Recognise that depression makes it hard for them to take the initiative. Be the loyal friend who will help them make that first step towards healing.

Shepherd of your flock,

I come to you in contrition.

For too long I failed to take seriously the phone calls, the texts, the emails which went unanswered, or too brief replies. In the busyness of my own life, I didn't notice that there was something seriously wrong.

I have been a poor friend to someone who had the right to think that I cared about them.

You never fail to notice the sheep which is missing from the flock. You are the woman who scours the floor for the one missing coin.

You have certainly noticed.

But now that I realize that all is not well, I am not certain what to do. I try visiting, but often there is no answer, or they have only just managed to drag themselves out of bed.

I feel helpless in the face of such hopelessness. The bright and friendly person I cared about has become someone I barely recognize.

Lord Jesus, grant me the compassion to accompany my friend through this dark hour. Give me the wisdom to say the right thing. If nothing I offer works, then may I just be there for them as they walk the valley of the shadow.

When prayer seems dry and meaningless to them, may they feel upheld by the raft of prayer from those of us who love them.

FAMILY

Depression is not like measles. It can take a while to realize that someone you live close to is ill. And depression is an illness, not just a persistent low mood.

Don't be afraid to speak the word out loud. It wasn't until one woman had depression herself that she discovered her beloved Nan, then in her eighties, had also suffered from it as a young woman. We urgently need to lift the stigma on mental illness by being open and truthful about it. There was a time when nobody uttered the word 'cancer'. Now, everyone is wearing pink ribbons and shaving their heads for charity.

So talk openly with the one you are caring for about their depression. They may or may not open up to you about the way they feel. They still need to know that you accept them for what they are, that you don't think less of them because they are ill. Assure them of your love and support.

The trouble with depression is that the very state blocks people from seeking the help they need or engaging in a lifestyle that will improve their outlook. You will need to be endlessly patient and understanding. You know there are positive steps they could take, but you can't force someone to take them.

Don't blame them for behaviour which seems self-destructive. Don't think less of them if they seem to wallow in self-pity. These are symptoms of genuine illness, just as much as a high temperature or a rash.

You are in the front line. It's not easy living with someone who has depression. You will need deep reserves of love.

Know that you are loved too.

Loving Father,

I know that your arms are around me. That you will never let me fall outside your love. Though I have done nothing to deserve it, it is your free gift.

Help me to find something of that boundless love for the one I care for, who is trapped in the mud of depression. May I fill them with the certainty that, whatever else goes wrong, I will always be here for them.

Give me the compassion to understand something of what they are feeling. Let me see how I can bring light into their darkness. When they reject the help I offer, may they still know that my support for them is solid.

I will need your help, day after day. I will need your patience, your humour, your perseverance. May my life and my love be a window through which they may see your love poured out for both of us.

'PULL YOURSELF TOGETHER'

Living with someone who has depression can be a challenge. They may stay up half the night, hunched over a screen, and then won't get out of bed all morning. They don't bother to dress properly. They spurn all your efforts to tempt them to eat well. If you try to get them to take some exercise, or to socialize, they put up a wall of resistance. You know they should see their doctor or contact a helpline, but you just can't get them to do it. Sometimes it seems as if they don't *want* to get better.

Day after day, you try to be patient and understanding. Then you can't stand their lethargy any longer and you crack. *'Make an effort!'*

You know you shouldn't. You feel guilty. You, too, are in danger of being overwhelmed by despair.

Hang on to the thought that the one you care about is ill. All these challenging behaviours are symptoms of that.

They may suffer from night terrors. They may stay up because they are afraid to go to sleep. They are almost certainly suffering from lack of self-worth and fear of failure. They think they are unpopular, that people are laughing at them behind their back. They are scared of going into company in case it reinforces these perceptions. Their sullen behaviour may trigger just the reaction they are afraid of. The outside world has become a threatening place. They want to take refuge under the blankets, but even that doesn't feel safe.

Hang in there. Their state of depression may not be uniformly bad. There may be chinks of daylight when you can get a positive response. Don't give up trying – and praying.

Try experimenting with music. This can have a positive

effect on mood. You may find that some styles of music work better than others. Show them your own enjoyment.

You may find that some things trigger particularly bad episodes, while other seems to lift the curtain a little. Use this knowledge.

Above all, don't say, *'Snap out of it!'* But you knew that, didn't you?

Patient God, who has never given up on humankind,

give me the same loving heart.

Let me not fall into the trap of thinking that I am the victim.

Fill me with your endless patience. May your Holy Spirit illuminate me with imagination to offer just the help the other needs. Let me be attentive to their moods, their needs, their fears. May I be the solid rock they can depend on.

May I have the wisdom to hold out a helping hand, to seize the rare opportunity when I can coax them to take exercise, food, to go out into company, to seek help and healing. May I enable them to see that there *is* a door out of their present suffering. Let me inspire them with courage to take the first step through it.

In all my efforts, gift me with humour and self-knowledge. Forgive me when my patience cracks.

Be patient with both of us.

THE COMPASSIONATE FRIEND

It is in the nature of depression that, when you most need prayer, it is difficult to have an awareness of God's presence. A sense of hopelessness makes you feel that nothing is going to make a difference.

This is where friends are vital. We can make the prayers they cannot. Our prayers for them can weave the net that stops them falling. The simple knowledge that others care enough for them to pray for them can be a step towards restoring their self-esteem.

Individuals with depression will differ on whether they wish their names to be added to a public prayer list, or whether they are reluctant to admit they are in need. We have to act sensitively, in accordance with their wishes.

The prayers of friends are essential. Yet we need to guard against thinking that, once we've prayed, we can wash our hands of any other involvement. Rather, our prayers should stimulate us seek out other ways we can offer help.

Often, God calls us to be the answer to our own prayers.

Christ, who has been my constant Friend and Companion,

I appeal to you for my friend in need.

Now, at the lowest point of their depression, they need you as never before. Yet the gloom of their condition may shut out the realisation of your presence. Prayer seems dry and unanswered. Nothing seems worth the effort.

Lord of the friendless, take my own prayers on their behalf. Grant them the knowledge that the arms of love are around them. Assure them that they are cared for and valued.

Give grace to the people who live closest to them. You know better than I do that depression of a family member or a housemate can be wearing for them too. Fill them with patience and understanding. Give them wisdom to offer timely encouragement and advice, and not to give up when it is rejected.

Let our love, like yours, be freely and endlessly given, not something that needs to be earned.

In their darkest hour, bring them hope and healing.

Use me.

LISTENING

One of the most helpful treatments for depression is talking therapy. This involves a professional encouraging someone with depression to talk through their problems one to one, or in a group.

Someone with depression may resist seeking help from a professional. Or resources may be stretched, so that there is a long waiting list for this therapy.

But there are always friends or family members. You don't need to be trained to lend a sympathetic ear — though it helps if you read up on the subject.

Don't make it obvious that you are trying to 'do good' to them. Depression often makes people withdraw into themselves. Lead the conversation round to it naturally. Don't give up. If necessary, chat away yourself, not requiring an answer. Watch out for subjects which elicit a response.

Make it clear that you are on their side. You may be tempted to blame their own behaviour for some of the problems which have led to depression, but keep this to yourself. They need all the love and understanding they can get. Being judgmental will be counter-productive.

And don't be too quick to pile on the advice, however much you are itching to do so. Save your exhortations about food and exercise, etc., for times other than this deeper conversation.

Above all, listen. You can use supplementary questions to draw your friend out more, but encourage them to do most of the talking. The mere fact of getting things off their chest will help. And a caring listener may find themselves tapping into things which the other has long buried, which may be the root cause of their depression. Some painful episode in their past, perhaps.

And respect the confidentiality of this conversation absolutely. They need to trust you.

Friend of the friendless,

you had a keen eye for those whom society rejected.

You saw Zacchaeus, whose need drove him to listen from the sycamore tree. Look with compassion on my friend who needs you now.

You know how inadequate I feel against the weight of this despair. I'm not trained for this; I feel out of my depth. Yet I am here, and I'm their friend. That's all that counts.

Give me the wisdom, the imagination, the sensitivity to start the conversation that will allow them to unburden themselves.

Let me not lose heart when they reject my attempts. Make me a willing listener. Hold back my ready tongue from glib advice or exhortations. May I be the trustworthy friend to whom they can confide what they have told no one else.

Let me be worthy to carry this precious knowledge in your name. When the talking is done, and the time is ripe to offer advice, may I choose my words well. Yet even if I am rejected, may I rest in your assurance that the talking itself has helped.

FRIENDS

Depression typically makes people withdraw from society. They feel worthless, they fear that others are laughing at them.

It's easy to let former friends slip out of your social circle and hardly notice it. You may comment that you haven't seen so-and-so for a while. But it may take some time before you wake up and realize something is seriously wrong.

Now is the time when your friendship will be put to the test. How concerned are you, really? How much of an effort are you willing to make to help?

First, make some serious enquiries from those who know them better. If you find that this person is showing signs of depression, what can you do?

You need to recognize that not wishing to socialize is part of that illness. Inviting them to meet up with the gang as they used to is probably not going to work.

Take the time to care for them individually. Respect how they feel about not going out into company. Think if there are other things you can do to give them pleasure.

It's hard for anyone not to feel cheered by a gift of chocolates, flowers or tempting cakes. But perhaps go easy on wine or beer. You don't want to encourage drug dependency in these circumstances.

Your friend may have lost the initiative to go out on their own, but you could offer to take them somewhere nice. Just the two of you. A local beauty spot, a concert, a pleasant but undemanding stroll.

If loss of income has compounded the problem, you could be the good angel who offers treats.

Don't pile on advice, even though you can see they

need it. Be the one who lifts their spirits.

Be prepared for rejection. The hopelessness they feel may make them turn away your efforts to help. Don't give up on them. Depression is not necessarily a uniform condition of gloom. They may have good days and bad days. Sooner or later, you are likely to hit upon a time when you get an unexpected 'yes'. Make the most of it. Have fun yourself, and hope that your joy will be infectious.

Keep coming back.

Christ, who called us friends,

may I be the friend who is needed in this dark time.

Alert me to the absence of one who used to be part of our group. Make me sensitive to their changes in behaviour.

When I see the signs of depression, grant me wisdom to see what I can do to help. If there are ways to lighten the gloom they feel, may I be the one to offer this.

Grant me perseverance when my offers are rejected. May they feel the love which keeps bringing me back. May I offer the small things that make a difference: the joy of colour, music, little luxuries.

May mine be the warmth and strength giving them the courage to venture out into what they perceive as a hostile world.

May I bring joy into a life that has lost it.

KEEPING CONTACT

You have a busy social life. Your phone is buzzing with tweets and texts. You enjoy meeting up with friends. It's easy to miss the fact that one of these friends isn't contacting you any more. You haven't seen them lately.

If you realise that you haven't seen a friend, or heard from them in a while, be concerned. There is a real possibility that something is wrong.

Take the initiative. Give them a call. If they are not picking up, leave a message. Ask if they're OK. If they don't get back to you, try a text or email. Show them you care about them.

Ask around. Are others having the same experience? If someone has dropped out of your social circle, they may be suffering from depression, which makes them want to withdraw.

They need your love and support. Their condition may make them reject overtures of friendship, but that doesn't mean they don't really want these.

They may be feeling a loss of self-worth. Something may have happened which makes them feel others are laughing at them. Assure them how much you value them. Tell them you miss them. Go and visit them, and don't be put off if they turn you away.

They need persistent love. Go·on with the texts and the tweets. These can be lighthearted, not requiring an answer. You're continuing to keep them in the circle of your friends. They will know you are still there for them.

If you can't visit them, at least call them once a week. Don't give up on them.

Alert the rest of your friends to your concern. Ask them to do the same. You don't want to bombard the one with depression with an unrealistic deluge of messages, yet you need to keep up a constant reminder that you all care about them, and want them back.

Make your love real.

Compassionate Saviour,

you cared for your friends even to the last. When you saw that they were weary with working for you, you took them away to rest. At the Last Supper, you promised them the continuing presence of your Holy Spirit. On the cross, you looked down at your mother and your friend and disciple John and gave them comfort from each other.

Touch our hearts now for our friend in need. May we go on enfolding them in our circle of love and friendship.

Help us to understand the condition of depression better, so that we view its symptoms with greater sympathy and see more clearly what we can do to help.

Save us from being shallow and fair-weather friends. Let us always be there for each other in the hard times. Let us not give up when we seem to be rejected. May our love be a rock they can rely on.

In our busy lives, may we never forget the one who isn't there.

May we assure them often that we love them.

SUPPORTING THE FAMILY

Severe depression can take a heavy toll on the rest of the family.

It's hard to live with someone who doesn't seem to want to get better. Their constant gloom and unhappiness hangs over the house. Other family members can feel guilty about their own enjoyment of life.

The lethargy that often accompanies depression means that they no longer take good care of themselves. They are unlikely to pull their weight around the house. More work falls on those who share it with them.

A common symptom of depression is a lack of interest in sex. Their partner's attempts to offer physical comfort may be rebuffed. The partner's own desires are frustrated.

A parent's depression can be bewildering for children. They don't understand this change in behaviour. It feels as though the love they depended on is being withdrawn. This can make a child feel frightened and needy.

A good friend will want to help someone in the grip of depression. But they can also offer help to the rest of the household. Make sure their partner has time out away from this. They need to have fun and relaxation, a chance to talk about their side of the situation.

You may be able to step in and offer something of the parenting the children are missing. Be warm, funny. Suggest you take them out sometimes. Provide little treats.

Hold all of them in your prayers.

Holy Spirit, Comforter and Strengthener,

look with compassion on those who daily bear the burden of a near one's depression.

When they feel weighed down by this, may they know the warmth and strength of your presence. Give them the wisdom, the resilience they need to cope.

Give grace to the partner who will suffer most from the change in the one they love. Grant them the loyalty to offer unfailing love. Guard them from the temptation to seek sexual comfort elsewhere.

Cast your loving wings over the children in this family. Heal the hurt they feel of care withdrawn. Give them friends who will shine the light of joy into their lives. Encourage their compassion for the one who used to care for them.

Bring healing to the one whose illness creates a gap in family life. May all of us who love them reach out to help.

Show me how I can play my part.

THE CARING COMMUNITY

If someone has been diagnosed with cancer or is going into hospital, we add them to our prayer list. If a family have been bereaved, it's obvious that they need our love and concern.

Depression is often a hidden illness. The symptoms are far less apparent. It doesn't have such a clear appeal to our sympathy.

We need to be sensitive to the fact that there will almost certainly be those among us suffering from depression. We need to be alert to the possibility.

It could happen following life-changes, such as bereavement, loss of a job, the breakdown of a relationship. We need to watch for changes of behaviour that could be due to depression.

When that happens, we need to be alongside that person, offering steady, non-judgmental friendship.

Ask them if they would like to be included on the church prayer list. There is no need to state publicly why someone needs prayer. If they are unwilling, there may be a prayer group or individuals you could ask to offer this support more discreetly.

Your church clergy, of course, will want to know and offer their own help. If your church has pastoral visitors, make sure the appropriate person has this information.

Be on the lookout. Don't let someone who is suffering slip through the net unnoticed.

God, who sees even a sparrow fall from the nest,

may we not be a community in which those among us suffer unheeded.

Make us aware of the many situations that can tip someone into depression. May we be watchful for those who have slipped out of our fellowship, or become withdrawn.

Let us be there for them, holding out the hand of friendship and support. May they know that our love is constant, even if they reject our offers of help. When their condition makes it hard for them to pray, assure them that we carry them in our own prayers.

Let us not be content with the easy friendships of our community. Give us the grace to persevere with those who walk a harder road. As you noticed the one sheep that had gone missing, and went after it, so may we seek out in love those who have slipped out of our fellowship and struggle alone.

Give us your heart of love.

DANGER TIMES

A caring community will know that there are certain times when people are in particular need of prayer and love. Bereavement, the loss of a job, the break-up of a relationship can not only be painful, but triggers to depression. We need to watch over those people, not just for days and weeks, but for months to come. It may take time for depression to overwhelm someone.

But there are other life changes which can bring about depression in circumstances when we might not expect it.

Many young people go off to university full of hope. They enjoy the social life, the study of their favourite subject, the greater freedom. But others feel overwhelmed by it all. They look at others who seem more popular and successful than they are. They struggle with new ways of learning and daunting work-loads. They miss their home and friends.

It's not easy to keep in touch when someone has moved away. Ask family and friends. Are they all right? Do they seem to be enjoying their new life? Catch up with them when they are home on vacation.

Make friends with new students who come to your area. Be mindful of what some of them may be experiencing.

It's the same with a new job. It may be great to get a promotion. Then the reality of the new post sinks in. Greater responsibilities may weigh heavily on them. Their boss and their colleagues may change, and the new relationships may not always work out well.

Again, be attentive to changes in behaviour, to unexpected absences from social events. People may no longer communicate the way they used to.

Moving house can be traumatic. They may lose the social network they relied on in the past. They may find a greater financial commitment harder to sustain. A different pattern of commuting may not be working out well.

Friends and pastoral workers need to be alert to these possibilities. You may not have been particularly close to these people, or they may be new to your community. You will need to be the one to reach out the hand of friendship.

Hold these people in your prayers.

Christ of the Holy Family,

you amaze us by telling your followers that we are your mother, your father, your brother, your sister. Help us to make your family in Christ a reality.

Make us a noticing community. Make us knowledgeable about the causes of depression. Help us to be watchful over those in our community most at risk.

Overcome our diffidence. Grant us the grace to reach out to someone in need, even if we don't know them well. Let us offer simple acts of friendship, words of concern.

Make us constant in prayer. Let those in need know that the warmth of our support is always there for them. When they are tempted by despair or lethargy, may they know that we have hope for them.

We could not walk our own journey without you at our side. May we always have the time and the perception to be there for others.

FEARS OF SUICIDE

Depression is not a rational state. It is not uncommon for people to feel so low that they harm themselves. They may feel suicidal.

If you have someone close to you who is, or may be, thinking of taking their own life, you will want to give them all the help you can.

The majority of suicides are men, but it can happen to women too. One reason for the imbalance is that it is not considered 'manly' to confess to weakness. Feelings get bottled up inside until the lid blows.

Encourage the one you are worried about to talk about their feelings. Tell them that it's a lot more normal than they suppose. There are loads of other people going through the same experience. It doesn't mean that they are weaker or more unworthy than their friends.

Young people are acutely sensitive to social media. They may feel they are unpopular, increasing their lack of self-worth. Recruit their friends to build up their self-esteem.

These black thoughts may feel like a load that is never going to go away. Assure them that it's not a life sentence. People do get over depression and take up their normal lives again. It's a question of finding the right treatment and working their way through it.

Joining a group where they can talk honestly about the way they feel can help.

If you are seriously worried, make the Samaritans phone number easily available where they can see it.

It will be a strain on you too, to live with this fear. You also need support. Your doctor may be aware of this and offer help. There will be leaflets in the surgery waiting room telling you what support is available locally.

If you want the one you love to open up about their feelings, be prepared to do the same yourself.

Father of Mercy,

I'm frightened.

I pick up the paper and see the face of another young person who has taken their life.

I'm afraid I will be the next one who sees the police car draw up outside, meets the eyes of the officers bringing news they know I do not want to hear.

I don't seem able to get alongside the one who is so dear to me. I know they are harming themselves, that they've talked of suicide. It's not something I can reason them out of.

Dear God, provide the specialised help they need, and swiftly. I know how many others there are who need this aid. I know that resources are overstretched. Forgive the selfishness that asks that it should not be my child who falls through the net before help arrives.

Be with me as I watch and worry. May your loving arms be around both of us. If we talk to no one else, let us talk to you.

LOOKING AFTER YOURSELF

Living with someone who has depression can take a toll on you. You see things they could do to help their condition, but you just don't seem able to persuade them. It is tempting to become exasperated, even though you know you shouldn't.

It can be hard for someone with depression even to get out of bed. They are unlikely to offer a helping hand with work about the house. You feel that the burden is falling unfairly on you.

The perpetual air of gloom can wear you down. It's not easy to stay cheerful with someone who is so downbeat.

You understand that these are symptoms of illness. You sympathise. You wish with all your heart you could make things different. But the dark cloud is in danger of enveloping you too.

It's important that you care for yourself and your own mental well-being. You need to stay strong for the one you love.

Make a weekly plan to take some time out for your own enjoyment. You may feel guilty about having fun when the one with depression certainly isn't. But a positive role-model of what a healthy lifestyle looks like can be a plus. The last thing someone with depression needs is a house-mate who deepens the gloom.

Make it clear that you're not being selfish. You still love them and are sympathetic. Invite them to join you, even though you expect to be refused. Perhaps bring home a treat from such an outing.

Don't feel guilty. You are helping both of you.

There are also times when you need someone to look after you. Support workers and self-help groups are available for those caring for someone with depression. Make use of them. You don't need to carry this burden alone.

Enjoyment of life is one of the rich gifts of creation. Cherish it.

Christ, who warms the hearts of those who know you,

I praise you for all the things which give me joy.

I have seen the pain of others and tried to heal it. Yet I give thanks for the good things too. For exercise, which makes the body glow. For stillness when I sit and contemplate the wonder of your world around me. For the beauty of art and music and drama. For the fellowship of friends, for shared food and drink. For laughter, and a chance to let my hair down.

Let me cherish all these times. May I bring back a soul refreshed to care for the one who cannot yet rejoice as I do.

I thank you that there are those who care for me too. The burden I bear is not nearly as great as that of depression. But I am only human. I feel the need to escape at times from that load, or to share my problems with others.

I bless you for smiling on me when I do.

RESOURCES

Mind UK has an excellent website, which deals with many aspects of depression: its symptoms, causes, treatment and how to live as well as possible with it. www.mind.org.uk.

The information is also available as booklets. Mind Infoline: 0300 123 3393 and info@mind.org.uk. It includes a long list of helpful organisations and resources.

Depression UK is a self-help organisation for people with this condition. It has a number of local groups and a bi-monthly magazine. There are Pen-friend and Phone-friend schemes and an internet chat forum. www.depressionuk.org. info@depressionuk. org. Box D-UK, Self-Help Nottingham, Ormiston House, 32-36 Pelham Street, Nottingham NG1 2EG.

Samaritans are always available for people struggling to cope. You don't have to be suicidal. Helpline: 116 123 (free). www.samaritans.org. jo@samaritans.org. Freepost RSRB-KKBY-CYJK, PO Box 9090, Stirling FK8 2SA.

The NHS has leaflets about the help available in your area. Your GP can tell you more.

There are groups for people with specific needs, such as bereavement or student depression. See Mind Uk for further details.

These pages are left blank for your own prayers.